BEDROOMS AND PRIVATE SPACES

BEDROOMS AND

DESIGNER

PRIVATE SPACES

DREAMSCAPES

MARCIE STUCHIN AND
SUSAN ABRAMSON

PBC INTERNATIONAL, INC.

Distributor to the book trade in the United States and Canada
Rizzoli International Publications
through St. Martin's Press
175 Fifth Avenue
New York, NY 10010

Distributor to the art trade in the United States and Canada
PBC International, Inc.
One School Street
Glen Cove, NY 11542

Distributor throughout the rest of the world
Hearst Books International
1350 Avenue of the Americas
New York, NY 10019

LIBRARY OF CONGRESS CATALOGING-IN-PUBLICATION DATA

Stuchin, Marcie.
    Bedrooms and private spaces/Marcie Stuchin & Susan Abramson.
      p   cm.
    Includes index.
    ISBN 0-86636-476-5 (hb : alk. paper). —
    1. Bedrooms. 2. Personal space. 3. Interior decoration.
    I. Abramson, Susan. II. Title.
NK2117.B4S78 1997
747.7'7—dc20   97-18477
                                                   CIP

CAVEAT—Information in this text is believed accurate, and will pose
no problem for the student or casual reader. However, the author was
often constrained by information contained in signed release forms,
information that could have been in error or not included at all.
Any misinformation (or lack of information) is the result of failure
in these attestations. The author has done whatever is possible to
insure accuracy.

DESIGN BY BTD/ROBIN BENTZ

Color separation by Fine Arts Repro House Co., Ltd., H.K.
Printing and binding by South China Printing Co. (1988) Ltd., H.K.

10   9   8   7   6   5   4   3   2   1

Printed in Hong Kong

For Mom,
whose impeccable taste
and classic style continue
to inspire me.

— M. S.

To my parents,
Seymour and Janice Arkawy,
whose creative spirit will
always be with me.

— S. A.

CONTENTS

FOREWORD
THAD HAYES

Today's bedroom is a primary living space. "Hearth and home," the traditional moniker for domestic comfort, has been reinterpreted and the bedroom is center stage.

As contemporary culture has upped our stress quotient, we are turning toward home for rejuvenation. Our private living spaces have taken on a therapeutic role: Jacuzzis anchor the master bath, treadmills beckon aerobic workouts. We meditate. We are revitalized. The bedroom, in effect, constitutes a womb.

Social change has redefined our bedrooms. The exodus of women from the home into the workforce has yielded an impetus for "quality" family time. The parents' bedroom, off-limits to children in past decades, is now the hub of shared family activities. It is also an office sporting the latest high-tech amenities.

As our requirements for the multifunctional bedroom escalate, our wish for a beautiful room remains paramount. This, then, becomes the designer's challenge: to create a beautiful bedroom within the context of today's overwhelming and complex expectations. *Bedrooms and Private Spaces* reveals how top designers are meeting that challenge—often brilliantly.

INTRODUCTION

**MARCIE STUCHIN
AND SUSAN ABRAMSON**

Few residential environments invoke such appealing and intriguing images as the bedroom and its adjoining spaces. For the architect and interior designer, whose task it is to merge the client's personal requests with their own creative statement, the bedroom can be the most challenging room of all.

While there is no standard blueprint for the perfect bedroom, it is here, nonetheless, in these most intimate quarters, that the impact of design is felt every day. More time is spent in the bedroom—and its adjunct spaces—than any other room of the house. As a result, the finished space should be a private haven that functions just as well as, if not better than, the public rooms of the home. Through a combination of skillful architecture and inventive interior styling, the finished product can become a private retreat reflecting the client's personality and unique style of living.

As today's lifestyles become more complex and personal requirements more diverse, our bedrooms take on increasing importance. We require more and more from the room in which we sleep. It is here that we dress, watch television, listen to music, read a book, eat an occasional meal and surf the Web. It is also our refuge when we are ill. Yes, a bedroom can serve a multitude of purposes: it is at once an exercise studio and a seductive boudoir . . . a family gathering place and a home office. Its mirrors see us at our best and our worst, and its lighting provides the illumination to transform us from private to public being. The multiplicity of the bedroom's functions must be ideally suited to the client. And the versatility of design must broaden to meet the changing profile of tomorrow's bedroom spaces.

In this volume, some designs are rooted in tradition while others are fanciful and futuristic. Many pay homage to pure architectural influences while some are cleverly devoted to details. Despite obvious differences, the rooms pictured here incorporate many similarities; most demand a plan that serves myriad personal needs.

Bedrooms and Private Spaces showcases an eclectic selection of design reflecting a variety of current lifestyles. Today's bedroom may be a personal oasis—soft and welcoming; a media center—cybertech haven; a collector's showcase—highly personalized; a spa sanctuary—spiritual or hedonistic; or a luxurious retreat—an icon of glamour.

The bedrooms and adjoining spaces included in this volume comprise a guide to the most innovative spaces created by many leaders of the design world. Some rooms featured are rich and inviting; others spare and monastic. All, hopefully, are inspirational. Each room represents the designers' greatest challenge: to turn a client's dream into a reality, harmoniously blending personal expression with aesthetic function. These are the kinds of designs that inspire imaginative dreamscapes and will influence bedroom design for years to come.

INSPIRED BY

TRADITION

WHITE NIGHTS

D A V I D   H .   M I T C H E L L

Washington, D.C.

David Mitchell's client, a busy environmental lawyer based in Washington, D.C., spent her working hours submerged in hectic, high-powered surroundings. For her personal space, however, she desired an atmosphere that was calm, classic, and uncluttered. She specifically requested a mostly white bedroom to serve as

15

PREVIOUS SPREAD *The custom-designed metal bed was refinished six times until the correct "antique" white finish was achieved. Silk damask on the headboard and bed covering emphasizes richness and purity.*
RIGHT *The built-in custom closets are equipped with sliding glass doors that were sandblasted and etched in a classic trellis pattern. A unique, contemporary, sculptured light fixture rests on the antique Biedermeier side table.*
OPPOSITE *A large, turn-of-the-century, mirrored armoire lends weight and height to the room.*

**PHOTOGRAPHY BY
GORDON BEALL**

a pristine backdrop for a treasured collection of fine antiques inherited from her mother. The only structural changes were made to the closets; Mitchell moved them from one side of the room to the other to allow for greater depth.

TIMELESS ROMANCE

BARBARA, MICHAEL, AND LIZ ORENSTEIN

Southampton, New York

ABOVE *One of the nine floral patterns gracing the room adorns the upholstered English chair.*
OPPOSITE *A nineteenth-century, wrought-iron, four-poster bed dressed in crisp, white, scalloped linens holds court under the eaves.*

PHOTOGRAPHY BY LIZZIE HIMMEL

Barbara Orenstein designed this inviting guest room for the 1995 Rogers Memorial Library Southampton Showhouse to look as if it had belonged in this stately seaside cottage for generations. Indeed, her choice of furnishings, wallpaper, and carpeting were meant to evoke cozy English rooms with their softly welcoming and slightly romantic appeal.

All My Sins Remembered   Rosie Thomas

To enhance the room's innate architectural integrity, Orenstein added crown moldings and extended the eave over the antique bed, thereby creating an ample nook for the bed and its accompanying tables. She created walk-in closets to maximize hidden storage. A large French linen press provides a distinctive, more traditional place to store clothing.

As many as nine charming textile prints were employed throughout the setting to further characterize the timeless cottage feeling. The completed bedroom, which measures 16 feet by 17 feet, appears frozen in time, a quintessential romantic retreat. Its only competition lies in stunning ocean views framed by the enormous picture window.

OPPOSITE *A reproduction eighteenth-century dressing table hosts a sparkling assortment of antique bottles for the boudoir, as well as a nineteenth-century silver vanity set.*
RIGHT *An enormous, painted French linen press empowers the room and emphasizes the height of the ceiling.*

BEACHSIDE BARNRAISING

GREG JORDAN

Wainscott, New York

When an investment banker purchased an old barn facing the Atlantic Ocean at the eastern tip of Long Island, he enlisted New York designer Greg Jordan to help transform his charming but inefficient space into a country home worthy of his vast collection of Southwestern paintings, Frederic Remington bronzes, and old Mexican furniture. The barn needed a complete renovation not only to enhance specific living requirements, but also to maximize outstanding ocean views not revealed by prior alterations. Jordan's total "gut" job eliminated virtually all of the small interior rooms

and simplified the living plan into fewer, but larger, spaces with grand windows showcasing magnificent, previously hidden, water views.

The warm colors of the barn were dictated by the intense hues of Southwestern paintings, but Jordan was requested not to mimic the Pueblo adobe style. Instead, he set a decidedly polished, though casual, European tone. To age the newly Sheetrocked walls, Jordan commissioned local artisans to hand-trowel a mud of plaster and crushed marble dust. All banisters were hand-turned also to achieve an aged appearance. The overall effect is harmonious, old-world, and masculine, a picture-perfect East Coast backdrop for a carefully chosen collection of Western art.

SYMPHONY SPACE

DAVID H. MITCHELL

Chevy Chase, Maryland

David H. Mitchell Associates saw promise in what was considered the least appealing room in the National Symphony Orchestra's 1995 Chevy Chase, Maryland, showhouse. The 12-foot by 12-foot space was totally nonsymmetrical, but what the room lacked in equipoise it made up for in light.

OPPOSITE *The textures and patterns found in the fabric on bedding, wallcovering, and furniture emphasize the freshness and purity of nature. Fluid lines of a custom tray table complement the strong verticality of the slim four-poster and tall easel.*
RIGHT *An apple-green window shade and throw pillow on the white chaise frame a lush canopy of trees and bring in the outdoors. A botanical motif repeated in the legs of the side table continues the naturalist theme.*

PHOTOGRAPHY BY WALTER SMALLING

To camouflage myriad imperfections, the design team used warm, bright neutrals for the walls, furniture, and floor coverings, capturing an abundance of sunshine. The mix of furnishings, artworks, and vibrant splashes of organic color provide further distraction from the room's inherent flaws. Apple-green accents on windows and pillows

OPPOSITE *A gingham comforter, tapestry folding screen, and sturdy custom four-poster bed are strong yet romantic design elements.*

LEFT *Crisp white sheets show off two decorative shams. Their arabesque pattern is repeated in the folding tapestry screen. Topping a custom pine bedside table is a playful tea service.*

made from iridescent cotton fabric enliven the space. Similarly, Russian botanical prints cleverly perched on floating easels reinforce a naturalist sensibility. Warm, dark woods, used liberally for the bed, tray table, desk and easels, punctuate the bright backdrop and appear sculptural and important. The overall effect is a harmonious blend of light, warmth, and gentle movement. It is a composition in contrast, at once modern and traditional and altogether thoroughly successful.

LEFT *Above the fireplace hangs an oak medallion depicting a Roman wreath. A trio of grassy planters maintains the fresh outdoor theme.*

RIGHT AND OPPOSITE *A monogrammed slipcover in off-white damask weave personalizes an upholstered club chair. The custom-designed, two-tone, 21-drawer pyramid desk makes a bold and towering statement against the striped wall covering.*

SITTING PRETTY

BARBARA AND MICHAEL ORENSTEIN

New York, New York

As partners in their home-based design firm, Barbara and Michael Orenstein combined living with working in their New York City apartment. With space at a premium and their two daughters away at college, they transformed their personal quarters into a showcase of design to serve their many business and personal needs.

PREVIOUS SPREAD *The Orenstein's bedroom is a personal tribute to the "English Country style," exemplified by an easy mix of chintz fabric in warm pastel tones combined with favorite personal objects and carefully selected antiques.*

RIGHT *A close-up of the brass footboard shows an intricate inlaid medallion.*

PHOTOGRAPHY BY
MICHAEL MUNDY

Barbara Orenstein wanted her dramatic master bedroom to include a romantic salon where she could quietly retreat at the end of the day. In order to accommodate the inviting love seat and armchairs within the small dimensions of the bedroom, the furniture needed to be scaled down. Adjacent to the sitting area, an eighteenth-century English mahogany secretary serves both as a writing desk and as a multipurpose storage piece.

OPPOSITE *A delicate lace half-tester crowns the early-nineteenth-century French brass bed. Afternoon tea can be served from the plump ottoman in the adjacent sitting area. The floral needlepoint rug is Portuguese.*

P U R E L Y

ARCHITECTURAL

A MOUNTAIN RETREAT

DAVID COLEMAN

Vermont

For a New York couple looking for a romantic vacation home in the New England mountains, architect David Coleman designed a classic structure that enhances the natural beauty of the environment and infuses it with modern form and detail. The home, carefully situated in its pastoral setting, obtains maximum views of the surrounding Vermont countryside.

The home's warm interior draws from the rich splendor of nature's elements. In the master bedroom suite, a cathedral-like ceiling and broad expanse of windows express the grandeur of the surroundings. Neutral furnishings harmonize with the colors of the outdoors.

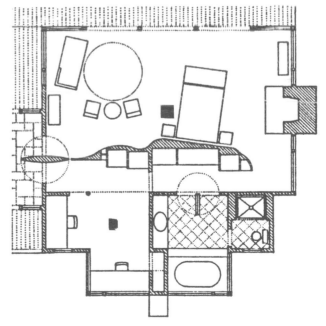

OPPOSITE *The beauty of the mahogany floor and the ebonized baseboard enhances the simplicity of the study's geometric lines.*
FOLLOWING SPREAD *David Coleman's canopy bed appears to frame his maple cabinet as well as the sitting area. Italian task lights illuminate the bed for reading once the abundant natural daylight fades to darkness.*

ATTIC SUITE

MARK McINTURFF

Washington, D.C.

Families who reside in row houses are all too familiar with their problems: rooms laid out like narrow railroad cars typically do not offer sufficient sunlight or space and they sorely lack for privacy. The clever renovation of this three-unit structure by Mark McInturff, an architect based in Bethesda, Maryland, completely redefined the style and functionality of this conventional row house in Washington, D.C.

RIGHT *A first glimpse into the master suite reveals the bed situated under an eave beneath a verdigris arch.* **OPPOSITE** *The opposite gabled wall with its doorway leading to the new balcony is situated behind the archway. Architect Mark McInturff added this form to balance the one in the niche above the bed.*

PHOTOGRAPHY BY MARK McINTURFF, JULIA HEINE, AND ROBERT LAUTMAN

McInturff first enlarged the ground floor, adding a wall of gabled windows to maximize light. His crowning achievement, however, was the conversion of the formerly unoccupied attic into the master suite. The area already possessed classic architectural elements: towering height as well as generous width and length. Furthermore, natural light flowed in from the dormer windows. McInturff divided the long space into three distinct areas for sleeping, sitting, and exercising. He also added another gabled window with access to a new balcony.

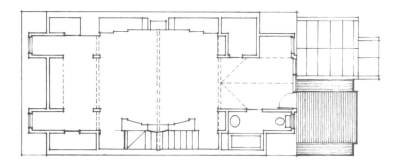

OPPOSITE *A full view of the maple wall panels and fireplace with marble steps can be seen from the sitting area.*
BELOW *Maple dressers are inset and topped with marble. A geometric verdigris railing, seen from the stairwell on the other side, continues the linear pattern of the dressers and wall panels.*

CALIFORNIA DREAMING

STEVEN EHRLICH

Santa Monica, California

ABOVE *Architect Steven Ehrlich's advanced geometry creates a structural frame for scenic, serene dreamscapes.*
OPPOSITE *The monochromatic whitewash of the bedroom and its furnishings blends with the sun-bleached vistas beyond. Exposed horizontal tie rods support the walls.*

PHOTOGRAPHY BY GREY CRAWFORD

Modernist architect Steven Ehrlich is well-known for his ability to fuse the indoors with the outdoors. In his design for a Santa Monica beach house, he deftly brought the invigorating sights and sounds of the ocean into the expansive setting of this bold composition, where they create a strong, satisfying presence. In the master bedroom, for instance, to dissolve barriers between interior and exterior and to pro-

OPPOSITE *At twilight, the bed, also of Steven Ehrlich's design, is accentuated by its ethereal, gauzy canopy. Two built-in storage units symmetrically flank the wall of windows.*
BELOW *Decorative vintage pillows soften the room's geometric shapes and provide a nostalgic hint of color.*

duce a sense of transparency against the beach and sky, the western wall is constructed entirely of glass.

The bedroom's dramatic geometry was integrated with the uncluttered simplicity of the furnishings. The room's dreamy white washes accentuate the even whiter forms of its free-flowing space. Throughout, small built-in cabinets fulfill the client's need for organized storage.

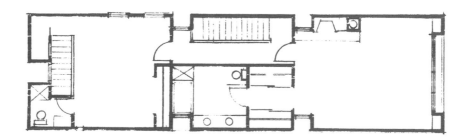

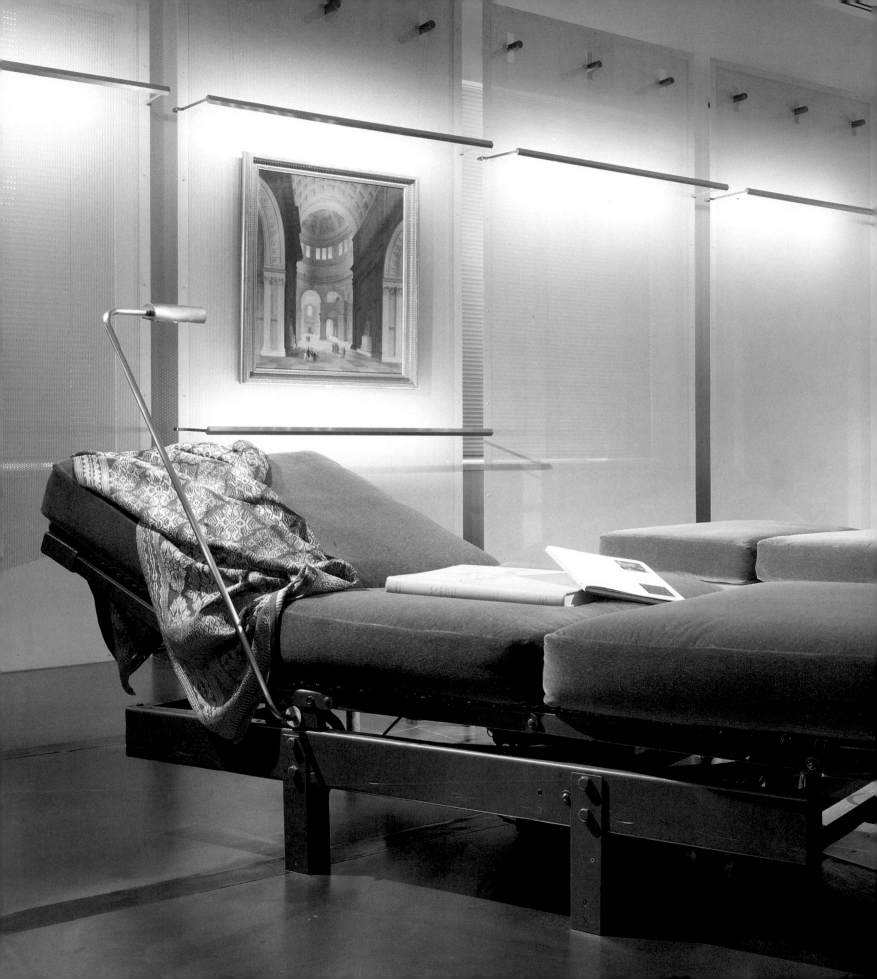

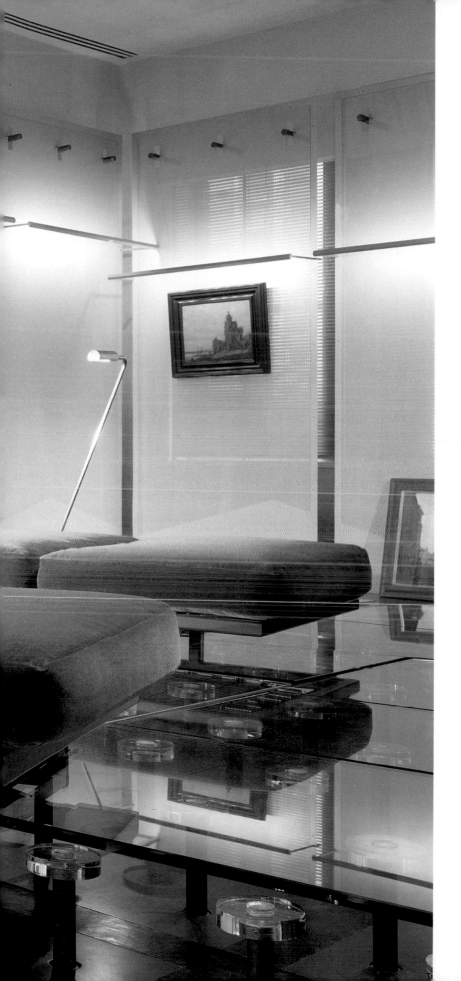

A SHOWCASE FOR ART

**JEFFREY PARSONS AND
MANUEL FERNANDEZ-CASTELEIRO**

New York, New York

An avid art collector well-versed in the language of design, the client of New York architects Jeffrey Parsons and Manuel Fernandez-Casteleiro requested that the renovation of his residence serve to accommodate not only his guests but his remarkable art collection. The resulting reconfiguration uniquely addresses both of these considera-

PREVIOUS SPREAD *Two movable daybeds can glide along a raised glass platform. The glass allows light into the interior and is strong enough to support the weight of several people.* **RIGHT** *A sturdy stone base supports the cantilevered glass writing desk.* **OPPOSITE** *Perforated and electrified metal panels for filtering daylight and illuminating artworks line two sides of the room. Paintings are hung from pegs and lit by flexible light fixtures that can swivel and slide up and down the panels as needed.*

PHOTOGRAPHY BY PAUL WARCHOL

tions. Three large rooms, each with its own specific function and art pieces, adjoin a 65-foot-long spine or gallery. There is no formal bedroom, living room, or dining room, but rather, a "viewing room," a "conversation room," and a "studio." Each space was planned to serve innumerable practical as well as aesthetic demands.

When designing the interior, the architectural team explored new ways of using basic materials. Two experiments—a raised glass floor support system and electrified metal panels—were ingeniously utilized in the viewing room. This transitional space was intended as a backdrop for overnight guests to view a changing display of artworks.

ROMAN ARCHES

TRANSIT DESIGN

Rome, Italy

When Danilo Parizio of Transit Design began work on this three-floor apartment in a residential Roman "Villino," his idea was to open up new space without interfering with the original shape of the structure. Designed in the early 1900s, the building contained lofty ceilings characteristic of Italian architecture and a series of arches reminiscent of ancient Rome.

RIGHT *Mirrored closet doors magnify the area at the top of the bedroom landing.*
OPPOSITE *Studio Transit designed the furnishings for the master bedroom using black to define the neutral space.*

PHOTOGRAPHY BY JANOS GRAPOW

ABOVE *Looking through the arches, the curved stairway leads to a new intermediate level. The whiteness of the walls is briefly interrupted by a primitive sculpture. Black steel hardware elegantly complements the architectural elements of the building.*

Parizio's goal was to create more closets and storage as well as a fitness area. The solution was to build an intermediate level in the private area of the apartment and connect it to the existing floors by a spiral staircase. The result was a whole new floor containing multifunctional walk-in closets and an area for workouts.

ABOVE *A postmodern boudoir—updated for today's sports enthusiast!*

RIGHT *Rows of shelves and built-in drawers in the walk-in closet of the master bedroom will satisfy even the most avid shoe collector.*

RIGHT *The trellised terrace—a very private sauna just a stone's throw from the city—as seen from the bedroom.*
BELOW *An arched doorway frames a view of the terrace from the master bedroom.*
OPPOSITE *Billowing white cotton canvas shades an intimate alfresco breakast area from the blazing Roman sun.*

CELEBRATING COLOR

SHOCK TREATMENT

D A V I D   H .   M I T C H E L L

McLean, Virginia

The narrow bedroom of a suburban Washington, D.C., tract mansion posed a challenge for David H. Mitchell. When designing this young man's room, his goal was to infuse a straightforward space with bolts of high energy. To achieve maximum impact, he chose color as his primary tool. Beginning with a basic black, white, and gray

PREVIOUS SPREAD *Black and white has never been so vibrant as it is here, providing drama to an otherwise mundane tract-house bedroom. Charcoal gray draperies shade the window wall while rubberized grommets slide effortlessly on rings along the brushed steel rod.*
LEFT *A brushed steel nightstand sets the stage for a geometric collage of accessories.*

PHOTOGRAPHY BY GORDON BEALL

palette, he completed the picture by introducing a shock of red for dramatic contrast.

Although Mitchell made no structural changes to the space, he was able to completely transform its appearance. An unlikely mix of hard-edged materials and soft textures—steel, silver leaf, and flannel—have ingeniously underscored the simple rectangular shape of the room. Generously proportioned furniture, grouped into functional vignettes, provides greater interest to the space.

ABOVE *Gray flannel draperies form a striking backdrop for the stained Shaker-style bed. Crisp white linens continue the theme of hard-edged tailoring and play up the shades of black and white in the photograph.*

ABOVE *Red stadium blankets create a robust counter-point as upholstery material for the tufted Victorian chair. The color is repeated in the buffalo-check throw pillow.*
OPPOSITE *An innovative, silver-leaf folding screen with a skateboard base provides a glamorous backdrop to a revolving still life.*

TECHNICOLOR ARCHAEOLOGY

A C E   A R C H I T E C T S

San Francisco, California

ABOVE *The edifice is divided into two separate town houses, one above the other. Bay Area architectural heritage is amusingly presented within its two floors.*
OPPOSITE *The bed is designed as an architectural complement to the room, echoing its shallow arches. Its nineteenth-century Amish quilt continues the triangular motif seen in the marble floor.*

PHOTOGRAPHY BY ALAN WEINTRAUB

David Weingarten of Ace Architects purchased this San Francisco building and spent three years constructing an extraordinary edifice whose unusual silhouette and whimsical mix of architectural styles produce a jarring contrast to the more sedate row houses nearby.

The vivid structure, which Weingarten designed for himself, is an inspired and imaginative retrospective of the three stylistic

stages of Bay Area architecture. This chronology is present throughout the house in myriad architectural references. Weingarten's archaeological explorations, consisting of a master bedroom and a terrace, begin on the lowest level, the "pre-historic" floor. Slate, a basic material, covers the terrace while the geometrically patterned marble on the bedroom floor suggests an ancient mosaic.

COLOR FORMS

STEVEN EHRLICH

Venice, California

A busy Hollywood executive with an impressive collection of art enlisted architect Steven Ehrlich to design her Venice, California, home. Beginning with a stark white backdrop, Ehrlich accentuated the powerful space with vivid slices of color. Using a variety of design elements in the bedroom suite, he created a room that is at

75

PREVIOUS SPREAD *The walls of the house were left white in order to accommodate the owner's art.*
RIGHT *Bands of square windows surround the bathroom, infusing it with light. White ceramic-tile walls and floor accent the honey-colored wood pedestals of the twin sinks.*

PHOTOGRAPHY BY
GREY CRAWFORD

once minimal yet monumental in its pro-portions, matching the intense colors of his client's art with those of his design.

The bedroom's focal point is the fireplace wall, a multilayered sculpture of mottled plaster that visually expands the sense of space. A grand-scaled mirror, chosen by the client, is carefully angled to reflect the room's multiple personalities. Graceful lines define the bed and storage chest, and com-plement the painting overhead. Paired pedestal sinks punctuate the tiled bathroom.

ABOVE *A delicate, rose-print bed cover balances the Eastern orientation of the furnishings. A walk-in closet adjacent to the bedroom serves most of the owner's storage needs while a whimsical clothes rack provides for easy access beside the bed.*

RHYTHM AND BLUES

ALFREDO DE VIDO

East Hampton, New York

Alfredo De Vido's design for an East Hampton residence presents an innovative approach to storage space in the master bedroom. Here, the architect and his design partner, Catherine De Vido, focused on form and function with the inventive, custom-made storage units and built-ins. Architecturally, they create a mood of tranquillity by employing an eclectic mix of styles, forms, and shapes.

RIGHT: *Strong blue notes accentuate the graceful curves of the chaise and rocker.*
OPPOSITE: *The bed, with its built-in canopy and sky blue coverlet, seems to levitate above the hardwood floor.*

PHOTOGRAPHY BY NORMAN MCGRATH AND RICHARD LEWIN

The bed, enthroned in a built-in canopy, became the room's focal point. Its presence was further enhanced by the artful use of the color blue. In the opposite corner, a large column repeats the strong blue theme. While it appears to have been built as a structural support, it is actually an ingenious floor-to-ceiling chest of drawers. Honey-colored woods and pale yellow walls provide a warm backdrop for the sober geometric lines of the furnishings. The overall effect is minimalist with a Zen-like harmony.

FORM AND
FUNCTION

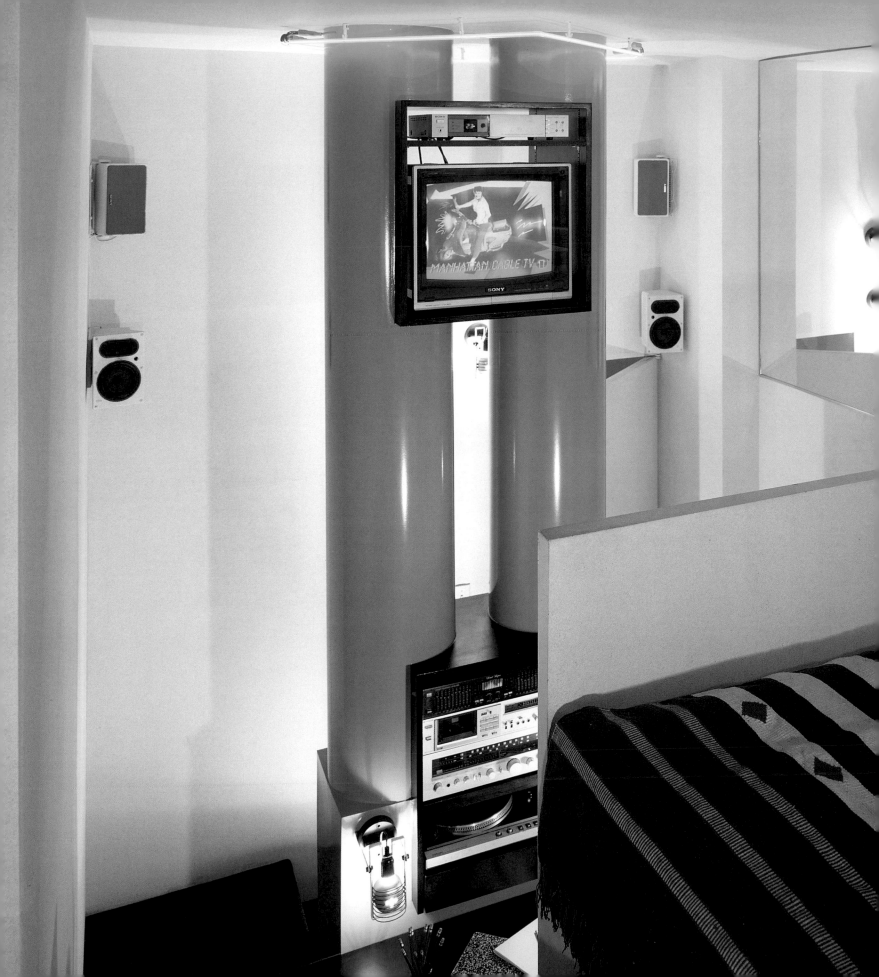

HIGH-TECH HAVEN

LEONARD BRAUNSCHWEIGER

New York, New York

This New York client needed nothing short of a magician to transform his gloomy 136-square-foot space into a brilliant, high-tech, teenager's lair. Architect Leonard Braunschweiger proved to be one. First, he completely reconfigured the room's meager proportions and capabilities by removing doors and a partition. Then he

LEFT *Suspended at eight feet, the television is placed within clear view of the sleeping loft.*

PHOTOGRAPHY BY DAVID SABAL

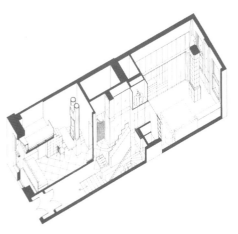

ABOVE *Extra seating is offered by the daybed, which also enjoys a full view of the television.* **RIGHT** *Electric-blue twin columns extend to the ceiling and enhance the illusion of great height while providing functional support for the television and stereo system.* **OPPOSITE** *A bold red staircase elegantly descends toward the base of the columns, incorporating additional storage. One of the steps was widened to 27 inches and covered in plastic laminate to serve as a unique desk.*

added a series of minimalist architectural elements that imbue the space with visual excitement. He used bright primary colors to define the geometric shapes of the functional supports and storage units. Finished, this formerly claustrophobic room seems almost expansive and easily serves a multitude of teen-age requisites.

FREUDIAN FANTASY

ACE ARCHITECTS

Berkeley, California

When two California psychologists hired Ace Architects to create a new master bedroom suite from three mundane rooms in their Craftsman-style home, their requests were fairly straightforward: a bedroom painted the colors of a Venetian sunset, an area for yoga that also had room for books, and a soothing, oasis-like bath. The clients' most fundamental requirement was

that the new spaces exemplify an intellectual study in contrast and contradiction.

Ace mastered these considerable challenges by presenting a design scheme full of architectural allegory and Freudian theory—a plan in which each remodeled room would represent one of Freud's three aspects of the self: the id, the ego, and the superego. A single circular axis connects all three rooms.

LEFT Strategically placed mirrored closets and a graceful curved desk embellish the austere dressing room, or "ego" space, used for yoga.

BELOW In the master bath or "id," a niche frames a painting celebrating female beauty. Random-patterned tiles and obscure lighting transform this former closet into a grotto-like bath.

OPPOSITE The artist and the designer created a classically composed mural for dreams and fantasy. The grandeur of the fluted colonnade draws the eye spiritually and visually upward.

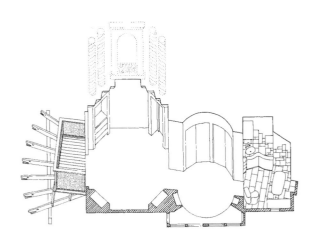

LUXURIOUS MINIMALISM

DUBAY AND MAIRE

Chicago, Illinois

To take advantage of its sweeping views both of Lake Michigan to the west and the historic, gold-coast neighborhood to its east, this apartment on prestigious Lake Shore Drive was completely reconfigured and opened up by Chicago-based architecture and design team DuBay and Maire. Eschewing the former labyrinth of narrow corridors and closets with partially obstructed vistas, DuBay and Maire provided

RIGHT *In the master bath, floors and walls of mocha-colored limestone, stainless steel cabinetry, and an unusual wall-mounted faucet underscore the rich, contemporary feeling of the apartment.*
OPPOSITE *The bed, headboard, and bedside table, all custom-designed by DuBay and Maire, were fabricated from unstained, bleached English sycamore. The headboard niche provides illuminated shelving for antiquities from the Douglas Dawson Gallery, Chicago.*

PHOTOGRAPHY BY TONY SOLURI

OPPOSITE *Sliding panels accented with lacquered color evoke minimalist paintings, but function to conceal closets.*
RIGHT *The sofa is covered in bronze-leaf leather adorned with throw pillows made of Persian lamb and stenciled pig skin. The pedestal table is polished aluminum and black leather.*

the apartment with a backbone, a "panelled" wall that bisects the linear space from east to west, affording a clean straight line to the windows.

To highlight the client's striking collection of art, neutral tones were used throughout.

Materials for the major pieces—leathers, panne velvet, fine silks, and fortuny cotton—are texturally rich and luxurious. The overall look is highly polished and elegantly minimal, all the more exceptional since its two designers are well-known traditionalists.

STREAMLINED STYLE

MOJO STUMER AND ASSOCIATES

New York, New York

The owners of this 14,000-square-foot, cedar and granite contemporary house nestled in a mountainside some 30 miles north of New York City had a long design "wish list," especially when it came to planning the 800-square-foot master bedroom suite. Aside from privacy, what they were

PREVIOUS SPREAD *Bleached ash was used for all of the cabinetry. The custom headboard, which runs the length of the wall, has curved angles encompassing night tables, shelving, and a desk. The bed and footboard are also encased in ash. Padded silk walls and billowing draperies complete the streamlined look. The Deco-inspired chair is by Donghia and the "French" club chair is by Koska. Chrome lighting fixtures complete the Deco reference.*

RIGHT, TOP *Mojo Stumer and Associates designed the chaise for the owner, a businessman/theater producer. It, too, echoes the graceful angles of the Deco era.*

RIGHT, BELOW *A 35-inch television lifts out of the footboard cabinetry on a swiveling shelf, where it can be seen from any viewpoint.*

PHOTOGRAPHY BY PHILLIP ENNIS

after was a soft, streamlined look, contemporary in style and elegant in demeanor. The overall effect recalls a sleek, king-size cabin on a 1940s ocean liner. Bleached ash cabinetry, luxuriously upholstered walls, and French-inspired furniture embellish this soft peach, modern bedroom with glamorous Deco allure.

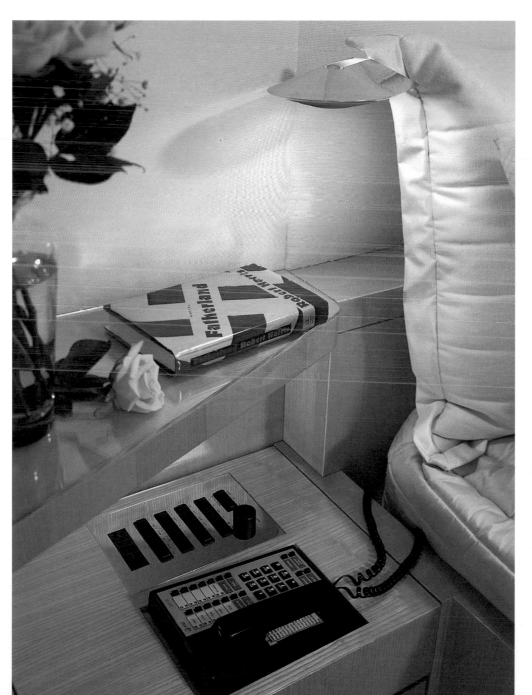

LEFT *Electronic bedside panels control all of the bedroom and bathroom lighting, as well as the stereo system and draperies.*

PERFECT PIED-À-TERRE

CLAUS RADEMACHER ARCHITECTS

New York, New York

Noted for stately town houses and handsome apartment buildings guarded by white-gloved doormen, the immaculate homes of Beekman Place reflect the essence of genteel New York style and polish. Architect Claus Rademacher kept the setting in mind when commissioned to design a pied-à-terre for a retired executive and his wife from San Juan, Puerto Rico, who planned on using the apartment as a second home. The

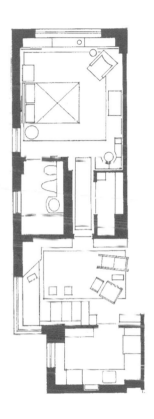

LEFT *The custom oak cabinetry in the sitting room perfectly illustrates the axiom "form follows function." Upholstered seating utilizes Randolph and Hein chenille fabric; the leather lounge chair is a Mies van der Rohe "MR" chair.*

clients' requests were direct; they desired a space radically different from their grand primary residence, an elegant urban shelter dictated by modernist simplicity and devoid of traditional architecture and old-world decorative treatments.

Rademacher's design for the apartment, which measures approximately 1,500 square feet, employs quarter-sawn, white oak custom cabinetry, both for utility and for spatial progression from room to room. Subtle variations of soft whites and beige tones quietly unify the apartment. Antiques are effectively juxtaposed against classic modern furniture for an overall atmosphere that is at once sophisticated, relaxing, and functional.

MODERNIST MASTER SUITE

PETER L. GLUCK AND PARTNERS

New York, New York

ichly elegant, simple, and accommodating were precisely Peter Gluck's directives when designing a new master suite for a young Manhattan couple. The project, part of a massive renovation and expansion of a large penthouse duplex, entailed installing a private elevator and staircase

RIGHT, TOP *The master suite boasts enormous storage potential hidden behind paneled Anegré doors.*
RIGHT, BOTTOM *A geometric panel extending from the headboard functions as wall-washer lighting.*
OPPOSITE *The bed niche is wrapped in sheets of Anegré wood in subtly varying grains. Well-placed recessed lighting warms the room.*

PHOTOGRAPHY BY PETER L. GLUCK

ABOVE *A modernist-inspired elliptical staircase leads to the third-floor master suite.*

linking the couple's existing two floors to a third level carved from the building's water tower compartment. To achieve this formidable goal, Gluck was required to completely re-engineer the water supply to the basement, which was outfitted with a new standpipe system and firefighting pumps.

The resulting suite, accessed via the private elevator or elliptical staircase, is a modernist's dream. Gluck expanded the apartment vertically, bringing light to the center of the home by opening the staircase to the ballroom above. His modernist theme continues throughout the renovation.

A VILLA TRANSFORMED

TRANSIT DESIGN

Martina Franca, Italy

On the southern coast of Italy lies the fairy-tale region of Puglia. It was here, near the coastal town of Martina Franca that Transit Design created this dramatic family vacation villa. The challenge for architect Danilo Parizio was to utilize the splendid form of the eighteenth-century country villa and transform it into a functional home for a twenty-first-century family of five.

RIGHT *The master bedroom is surrounded by frescoes of the "torn nuptial veil." Select furnishings and fabrics were chosen to complement the murals.*
OPPOSITE *Mid-height partitions successfully redefined the villa's interior, making the living space more compatible with the needs of contemporary family life.*

PHOTOGRAPHY BY
GIOVANNA PIEMONTI

The client wanted to retain the grandeur of the existing villa, complete with its cross-vault ceilings and original frescoes. Parizio's solution was to design a maze of mid-height, multifunctional partitions that would enhance, not hide, the ceilings. The handsome, screen-like partitions define space, create corridors, and provide walk-in closets and storage areas throughout the house.

OPPOSITE *A serpentine sweep of screens surrounds the master bedroom's dressing area, concealing intricate walk-in closets. The graceful curve of the neo-classical table is repeated in the terrazzo floor pattern.*

ABOVE *The bathroom is an elegant composition of glass, wood, and marble. A simple porcelain tub is given presence by its marble surround.*

RIGHT *Shelves in the daughter's room are built into the partitions, creating a showcase for a collection of antique urns and mandolins.*

JUST IN TIME

THE PASANELLA COMPANY

New York, New York

ABOVE *The custom-made cherry dressers with hooks afford a clever and convenient method for displaying a handsome collection of watches.*
OPPOSITE *Warm white walls and linens accentuate a pair of oiled cherry dressers used to store clothing and accessories.*

PHOTOGRAPHY BY PAUL WARCHOL

For a busy New York professional, finding affordable living space can be an onerous task. The job was even tougher for graphic designer Emily Oberman. As an avid collector of "stuff," from miniature cigarettes to Japanese chewing gum, she needed space to unpack her cartons and efficiently store and display their contents. She especially wanted to show off her collection of watches and clocks, many of her own design.

ABOVE, LEFT AND RIGHT *Videos are stored neatly in the bedroom on shelves below the television. Now you see it; now you don't. A mirror image replaces the television screen.*

With limited amounts of space to spare and money to spend, the client hired the Pasanella Company to design furnishings that could perform double-duty tasks. In the kitchen, they designed a large "picture frame" that ingeniously unfolds from the wall to become a table. The living room coffee table, constructed of open-sided storage cubes, can convert to a dining table. And in

OPPOSITE *A storage cube underscores a fine array of vintage clocks.*

RIGHT *When watching television in the bedroom, the mirror becomes part of the living room decor.*

the bedroom, they cleverly designed a pair of seven-drawer cherry dressers with hooks on top for hanging her watch collection.

Oberman's other passion, watching television, posed yet another design challenge. She wanted a television that could be seen from every room at any angle. Pasanella cut a square in the wall between the bedroom and the living room where the television could pivot on its base. A large mirror fastened to the back of the television allows the cut-out to double as a vanity.

PLANE GEOMETRY

THAD HAYES DESIGN

New York, New York

This apartment in one of New York City's finest landmark Deco buildings is a perfect example of Thad Hayes' craft. As requested by his client, a young anesthesiologist, the look is sophisticated and uncluttered, modern and practical. Its elegance is fostered by its simplicity. Rich, textural fab-

rics and highly polished woods establish a refined environment. Pared down to the very basics, every furnishing was carefully chosen and placed as an appealing backdrop for the client's collection of contemporary art.

In the peaceful environs of the bedroom, each piece of furniture projects weighty, almost sculptural, characteristics, and is meant to hold its own as part of the owner's collection of art and antiques. Hayes purposely kept the backdrop neutral to create a setting to showcase the art collection and provide an interesting juxtaposition of simple forms and luxurious materials.

OPPOSITE *The mahogany four-poster bed is custom-designed by Thad Hayes. Night tables are American Art Deco by Andrew Szoeke, circa 1934, and the bedside lamps are 1950s brass and ebony.*

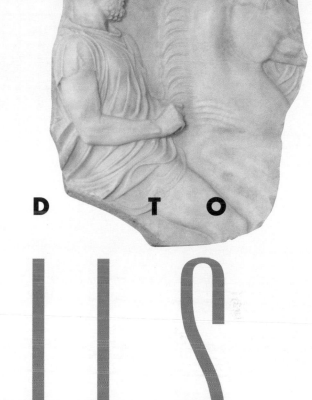

DEVOTED TO

DETAILS

A LESSON IN STYLE

SUTTA DUNAWAY

San Francisco, California

ABOVE *The bed linens, with their intriguing triangular border, are classic in pattern, natural in color, and understated.* **OPPOSITE** *The focal point of the room is the handsome steel bed with its bold geometric lines. A Biedermeier night table complements the rich paisley throw and echoes the warm tones used throughout.*

PHOTOGRAPHY BY DAVID LIVINGSTON

When West Coast designers Jula Sutta and Dan Dunaway planned this bedroom for a young man with a small but impressive collection of antiques, their goal was to create a warm, peaceful, sophisticated environment. Their choice of rich colors and materials—the patina of old wood, the crispness of tailored linens, the luxury of supple leather, and the strength of pure steel—lend the room an old-world charm while keeping the setting contemporary and youthful.

RIGHT *A Renaissance-style trestle table functions well both as a desk, and as a showcase for an eclectic array of small antiques.*
OPPOSITE *Voluminous silk drapes create a lush backdrop for a hip, ocher-colored leather chair and matching ottoman designed by Sutta Dunaway.*
BELOW *Subdued Umbrian tones provide a marked contrast to the hard edges of the four-poster bed, the sleek lines of the custom chair and ottoman, and the drum side table.*

BALANCING ACT

ANTONIA ASTORI

Milan, Italy

ABOVE *The gracefully curving leg of this monopode writing desk by Driade complements the Venetian glass vase.*

PHOTOGRAPHY BY MATTEO PIAZZA

The Art Nouveau architecture of a Milanese palazzo was the incentive for the renovation of this functional, modern apartment by architect and designer Antonia Astori. The clients, a married couple with an apartment in the palazzo, desired an elegant environment that balanced the delicate details of the original moldings, doors, and windows with the more practical elements of contemporary life.

The apartment's original parquet flooring and molded plaster ceiling remain intact. Their refined, geometric lines are enhanced by the Oniro bed and the Kora nightstand, both by Driade.

To achieve this goal, Astori enhanced the existing features with modern elements, created a fluid environment through the subtle use of neutral colors, and paid tribute to classic, early-twentieth-century bourgeois aesthetics and materials. Without modifying the structural shell, she organized the renovation around a singular, central corridor with a storage wall she designed to run its entire length, simultaneously unifying all areas of the apartment and satisfying utilitarian requirements.

RIGHT *The master bedroom as seen from down the hall. A Pompeiian-red plaster wall, framed by steel and glass, both integrates and separates living and dining areas.*

ABOVE *Architect Antonia Astori removed the original wall running through the central corridor, replacing it with a wall system of ocher lacquered Oikos storage units, her own design for Driade. The marble floor is original to the building.*

LEFT *The lush greenery of the palazzo's inner garden creates a dramatic backdrop for the master bath, while Bottiano marble enriches the neutral scheme.*

GUEST EXPECTATIONS

D A V I D   H .   M I T C H E L L

Washington, D.C.

David Mitchell's guest room for the 1994 National Symphony Orchestra Decorator Showhouse is a lesson in the mastery of monochromatic color and texture. A restrained palette of creamy tones counterbalances the sculptural quality of the furnishings and highlights their natural textures: the cool austerity of brass and iron, the sheen of polished wood and leather, the

RIGHT *A fluted leather chair from Donghia is placed next to a Native American drum table. Inspired by African carvings, Mitchell designed the armoire crafted of numerous rare woods.*

PHOTOGRAPHY BY WALTER SMALLING

ABOVE *Black iron and gleaming brass anchor the antique English bed and provide the room with a strong focal point. An orange cashmere throw is purposefully used as visual punctuation.*

ABOVE, LEFT *David Mitchell designed the bedside tables of cherry and birch. The pillow makes a bold geometric statement.*

ABOVE, RIGHT *Informal raffia on Donghia's St. James chair provides an unexpected contrast to elegant silk drapes.*

smoothness of silk, and the roughness of raffia fabric.

Although no structural changes were made to the 169-square-foot room, Mitchell's disciplined use of neutrals, offset by the green ceiling, enlarged and lightened the space. Preferring to give each piece plenty of breathing space, he created an overall environment that is spare, clean, and modern, yet still holds appeal for traditionalists.

ABOVE *Circle-back cane and mahogany chairs by Mariette Himes Gomez stand beside a table Mitchell created from a balustrade capped with white oak. Floor-to-ceiling silk drapes dramatize the room's height.*

WATERSIDE SERENITY

JOAN GRAY

Connecticut

Boundless views of sand, sea, and sky served as Joan Gray's inspiration for the complete transformation of a dark, two-story fishing cottage on the Connecticut shore into an airy, light-flooded, contemporary beach house. The client, a busy, single female executive, entrusted the entire project—including the choice of the renovation site as well as the architectural layout of the new structure and all of its details and furnishings—to Grayson Interior Design.

In accordance with strict building codes, Gray was required to keep the existing foundation and leave one wall standing. The project was therefore designated a renovation, rather than new construction. On the second floor, which housed the living area, rooms were combined and walls demolished, immediately opening up a large new

OPPOSITE *Sliding glass doors along the window wall open onto magnificent water views. The hand-cast aluminum basin, reflected in the mirrored wall, serves as a sink.*

LEFT *In the corner, a sunken tub was undermounted in the floor and surrounded by limestone tiles. The shower door, seen to the left, consists of two folding sheets of glass hinged at one end.*

space with soaring views of water on all sides. The layout downstairs remained essentially the same; the two bedrooms in the front were left structurally intact to serve as a guest room and an office or den.

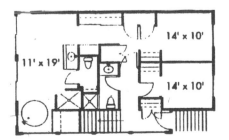

The two small bedrooms and bath in the rear of the house were merged to create one large, exciting bedroom. Enormous custom windows run the length of the back wall, maximizing the dazzling beach vistas. What emerged from the ruins of this renovation was a home unmistakably modern and functional highlighted by a spacious master suite—part sleeping spa, part Roman bath.

A GRISTMILL RESTORED

MATHIEU AND RAY

Saints, France

An abandoned gristmill outside Paris was the fanciful point of departure for this restoration by design duo Paul Mathieu and Michael Ray. Their client, a well-known Parisian bridal couturiere, was searching for both a tranquil retreat and an inspirational studio where she could create her romantic fantasies of tulle and lace.

Mathieu and Ray envisioned a space that was at once spatially minimalist and classi-

LEFT AND BELOW *The mahogany side tables were inspired by antique Viennese furniture. Custom torchieres of exotic wood and wrought iron are topped with parchment shades to illuminate the corners of the room.*

cally derived, but they first had to have the mill stripped to its bare structural shell. That which remained became the highlight of the master bedroom and the centerpiece of the

entire structure: the top floor of the mill housed remnants of the original grindstone and its rustic supports were transformed into the posts of a most intriguing bed.

OPPOSITE *Mosaic tile, wood paneling, glass and metal provide subtle variations of texture in the light, airy bathroom. Signature towel bars add a touch of whimsy.*

ABOVE *Centuries-old wood beams are seen in the designers' own studio.*

OPPOSITE *Original plank floors show off the elegant but spare furniture of the timeless design.*

PERSONAL
EXPRESSIONS

URBAN JUNGLE

SAMUEL BOTERO

New York, New York

W hen Samuel Botero discovered his Sutton Place apartment he never intended to live there very long—it measures a mere 450 square feet. But, empowered by the freedom that comes when designing for oneself, he envisioned his petite personal oasis. Murals would capture his fantasies and set the tone of the rooms: a jungle in his living room and an Egyptian desert in his bedroom.

Artists Patricia Kelly and Stephen Spera brought Botero's fantasies to life, setting the walls ablaze with color and exotic motifs. The backdrops, in combination with Botero's collection of South American arts and crafts and eccentric furniture, helped capture the very essence of primitive chic. The space, although tiny, has for many years provided the designer with the ultimate refuge from the stressful cosmopolitan "jungle."

OPPOSITE *Samuel Botero displays an eclectic personal collection of ancient artifacts, rare crystals, and a faux-Japanese lantern that he designed himself. He also inspired the circular painting with its gilt inset, intended as a spiritual symbol.*

RIGHT *Twilight descends in the "desert" (Samuel Botero's bedroom) when gold-leaf stars twinkle in the turquoise sky above sandstone-colored walls. Closet units are hidden behind murals copied from Egyptian tombs by painters Patricia Kelly and Stephen Spera. The lamp and bedside chest are also painted with ancient motifs.*

HOLLYWOOD HEIGHTS

RICHARD A. BEST

Hollywood, California

ABOVE *Perched on a hilltop, Best's contemporary house glows like an ornamental lantern in the twilight. The designer's preference for minimalism is evident in the cool geometry. High ceilings and abundant glass open the house to light and nature.* **OPPOSITE** *A row of clerestory windows on the side of the house nearest to its neighbors maximizes light yet assures privacy in the top-floor master bedroom. Shaker-style furnishings restate the building's purely architectural lines.*

PHOTOGRAPHY BY PHILIP CLAYTON-THOMPSON

A narrow, sharply sloped piece of land wedged high in the Hollywood Hills posed a steep challenge to architect Richard Best when designing his own home. His solution was to build four stories high, allowing magnificent outdoor vistas to merge naturally with the spacious interior design.

Best created a unique combination of public and private areas, placing his most private

space on the top floor. Here, the inviting master bedroom suite crowns the whole house, becoming the ultimate personal refuge. Warm woods, earth-toned textiles, and the enticing double fireplace in combination with the clean, dramatic lines of the architecture, maintain the emphasis on the outside view.

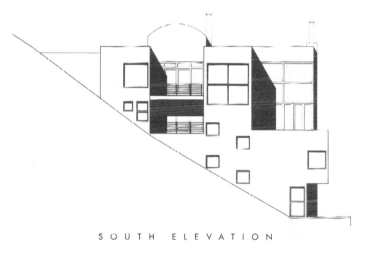

SOUTH ELEVATION

OPPOSITE *With simple luxury, the master bath's diagonal whirlpool tub shares the breathtaking view.*
ABOVE *Wall-to-wall mirror in the master bath reflects natural light. Smooth Carrara marble and a stainless steel sink replete with gooseneck faucet caps ash cabinetry.*
LEFT *The two-sided marble fireplace joins the master bedroom with a comfortable sitting room.*

RIGHT *The ease and comfort of the bedroom is refined and understated. Pale walls and rich stone are complemented by natural wood and set off by handwoven textiles.*

PUNCTUATION MARKS

THE TAYLOR & TAYLOR PARTNERSHIP

Miami Beach, Florida

William and Phyllis Taylor, an architect and a designer respectively, pooled their talents to create their own soothing retreat, which is a veritable work in progress. Operating on a limited budget, they first scoured estate and yard sales for furniture.

ABOVE *The contrast between the purity of gleaming white and the boldness of black is evidenced in the juxtaposition of the delicate embroidered bed cover and the powerful leather bergère and ottoman. Floral patterned details unify the open space.*

OPPOSITE *A nightstand, purposefully showcased against the pristine bed, displays the Taylors' collectibles and creates an artful vignette. The contrast of textures found in the primitive rattan trunk and the ancient patina of the old wood table reverberates against the smooth and creamy palette.*

PHOTOGRAPHY BY KEITH SCOTT MORTON

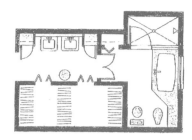

OPPOSITE *White is also featured in the bath, this time making a sharp, pure statement. Here, a more subtle contrast of cool gray marble heightens the brilliance of the white, while a gilded stand adds an element of surprise.*
RIGHT *The perfect private refuge is created by separating the bath and shower area from the rest of the bathroom. The repetition of white—in porcelain, tile, linen, and terry—is broken only by the accent of the needlepoint mat.*

Next, they layered a subtle array of polychromatic whites, punctuating them with unexpected, dramatic dashes of black. With their keen sense of detail, the Taylors satisfied their need for creativity; their serendipitous combinations of elements create a very personal space that is crisp and airy without being stark.

HOMEWORK IN CALIFORNIA

**GEOFFREY SCOTT
DESIGN ASSOCIATES**

Santa Monica, California

W hen architect Geoffrey Scott purchased this well-partitioned loft in Santa Monica, his goal was to create a large open studio which would accommodate both his personal living space and his professional design/furnishings showroom.

RIGHT *The bedroom is equipped with a system of sliding translucent panels.*
OPPOSITE *A custom nightstand is featured against a translucent, silk-screened hanging divider.*

PHOTOGRAPHY BY HUGO ROJAS

The renovation began with heavy demolition, which immediately made the space feel lighter and brighter. Old brick walls and rafters were left exposed, adding warmth and contrast to the cool white walls. Color and texture also play important roles in creating this visually exciting space.

OPPOSITE *A view across the loft space showcases the bedroom on the mezzanine level with a dressing area to the right. The design studio and furniture showroom are located on the ground level below.*

BELOW *Geoffrey Scott designed the custom furniture and lighting in the sitting area.*

MODERNO IN OLD TRASTEVERE

TRANSIT DESIGN

Rome, Italy

ABOVE *The long mirrored corridor provides hidden storage and leads to the master bath.* **OPPOSITE** *Bleached ash wood was used as a footboard for the platform bed, on the room's folding mirrored doors, and elsewhere throughout the apartment.*

PHOTOGRAPHY BY JANOS GRAPOW

Situated in one of the oldest sections of Rome, the Piazza Santa Maria in Trastevere has, in recent years, evolved into one of the most desirable neighborhoods in the city. Hundreds of centuries-old buildings have been rescued from the ravages of time and renovated to meet contemporary standards. While the exteriors have been cleaned up, they still uniformly project the

integrity of Rome's ancient architecture. The revamped interiors, however, are another story entirely.

Danilo Parizio, a partner in the architectural firm Transit Design, and his wife, an interior designer, had a strong desire to imbue their Roman penthouse apartment with architectural dignity while maintaining its ties to the historic buildings seen outside the numerous large windows. Connecting the two floors of the penthouse is a circular staircase designed by Danilo Parizio, who reconfigured the entire apartment from top to bottom to accommodate their busy urban lifestyle, as well as designed all of the furniture. The new home is light, airy, and boasts a number of ingenious hidden storage units.

All the windows were replaced during renovation, and throughout the home the couple installed several strategically placed mirrors to catch the natural light and highlight the extraordinary views of Trastevere.

DIRECTORY

Architects & Designers

ACE ARCHITECTS
David Weingarten
Lucia Howard
330 Second Street
Oakland, California 94607
United States
Tel: (510) 452-0775
Fax: (510) 452-1175

ALFREDO DE VIDO ASSOCIATES
Alfredo De Vido
Catherine De Vido
1044 Madison Avenue
New York, New York 10021
United States
Tel: (212) 517-6100
Fax: (212) 517-6103

ANTONIA ASTORI
Via Rossini 3
20122 Milan, Italy
Tel: (39) 2-795005
Fax: (39) 2-76021763

BARBARA ORENSTEIN INTERIORS
Barbara Orenstein
Liz Orenstein
Michael Orenstein
40 East 88th Street
New York, New York 10128
United States
Tel: (212) 534-2103
Fax: (212) 831-5076

RICHARD A. BEST
RICHARD A. BEST, ARCHITECT
1818 N. Sierra Bonita Ave.
Hollywood, California 90046
United States
Tel: (213) 845-4616
Fax: (213) 845-4751

SAMUEL BOTERO
SAMUEL BOTERO ASSOCIATES
420 East 54th Street, Suite 34G
New York, New York 10022
United States
Tel: (212) 935-5155
Fax: (212) 832-0714

LEONARD BRAUNSCHWEIGER
LEONARD BRAUNSCHWEIGER AND COMPANY, INC.
150 Fifth Avenue
New York, New York 10011
United States
Tel: (212) 242-1188
Fax: (212) 242-1866

CLAUS RADEMACHER ARCHITECTS
Claus Rademacher
Elizabeth Brosnan
136 East 73rd Street
New York, New York 10021
United States
Tel: (212) 535-1800
Fax: (212) 535-0829

DAVID COLEMAN
DAVID COLEMAN/ARCHITECTURE
1932 First Avenue, Suite 200
Seattle, Washington 98101
United States
Tel: (206) 443-5626
Fax: (206) 443-5626

DUBAY AND MAIRE
Daniel DuBay
Gregory Maire
445 N. Wells Street
Chicago, Illinois 60610
United States
Tel: (312) 222-0445
Fax: (312) 243-7611

STEVEN EHRLICH
STEVEN EHRLICH ARCHITECTS
2210 Colorado Avenue
Santa Monica, California 90404
United States
Tel: (310) 828-6700
Fax: (310) 828-7710

PETER L. GLUCK
PETER L. GLUCK AND PARTNERS
19 Union Square West
New York, New York 10003
United States
Tel: (212) 255-1876
Fax: (212) 633-0144

JOAN GRAY
GRAYSON INTERIOR DESIGN
266 Post Road East
Westport, Connecticut 06880
United States
Tel: (203) 222-7661
Fax: (203) 221-8263

THAD HAYES
THAD HAYES DESIGN
90 West Broadway, #2A
New York, New York 10007
United States
Tel: (212) 571-1234
Fax: (212) 571-1239

GREG JORDAN
GREG JORDAN, INC.
504 East 74th Street, #4W
New York, New York 10021
United States
Tel: (212) 570-4470
Fax: (212) 570-6660

ANNE LEEPSON
Grayson Construction
17 King's Highway North
Westport, Connecticut 06880
United States
Tel: (203) 221-7426
Fax: (203) 221-0924

MATHIEU AND RAY
Paul Mathieu
Michael Ray
12 rue Matheron
13100 Aix en Provence, France
Tel: 42 239 777
Fax: 42 239 759

MARK MCINTURFF
MCINTURFF ARCHITECTS
4220 Leeward Place
Bethesda, Maryland 20816
United States
Tel: (301) 229-3705
Fax: (301) 229-6380

DAVID H. MITCHELL
DAVID H. MITCHELL ASSOCIATES
1734 Connecticut Avenue, NW
Washington, DC 20009
United States
Tel: (202) 797-0780
Fax: (202) 797-9512

PARSONS AND FERNANDEZ-CASTELEIRO ARCHITECTS, P.C.
Jeffrey Parsons
Manuel Fernandez Casteleiro
62 White Street
New York, New York 10013
United States
Tel: (212) 431-4310
Fax: (212) 431-4496

THE PASANELLA COMPANY
Marco Pasanella
Alexander Brebner
45 West 18th Street
New York, New York 10011
United States

Tel: (212) 242-2002
Fax: (212) 242-2066

GEOFFREY SCOTT
GEOFFREY SCOTT DESIGN ASSOCIATES
2917 ½ Main Street
Santa Monica, California 90405
United States
Tel: (310) 396-5416
Fax: (310) 399-5246

MARK STUMER
MOJO STUMER AND ASSOCIATES
55 Bryant Avenue
Roslyn, New York 11576
United States
Tel: (516) 625-3344
Fax: (516) 625-3418

SUTTA DUNAWAY, INC.
Jula Sutta
Dan Dunaway
215 Crestview Drive
Orinda, California 94563
United States
Tel: (510) 253-0862
Fax: (510) 253-0868

THE TAYLOR & TAYLOR PARTNERSHIP
William C. Taylor
Phyllis Taylor
1631 Michigan Avenue
Miami Beach, Florida 33139
United States
Tel: (305) 534-9862
Fax: (305) 534-1582

TRANSIT DESIGN SRL
Giovanni Ascarelli
Maurizio Macciocchi
Danilo Parizio
Via Emilio Morosini, 17
00153 Rome
Italy
Tel: (39) 6-5899893
Fax: (39) 6-5898431

Photographers

GORDON BEALL
4507 Sagamore Road, #101
Bethesda, Maryland 20816
United States
Tel: (301) 229-0076

PHILIP CLAYTON-THOMPSON
7866 SE 16th Avenue, Portland, Oregon
United States
Tel: (503) 234-4883
Fax: (503) 234-5693

GREY CRAWFORD
139 North Union Avenue
Los Angeles, California 90026
United States
Tel: (213) 413-4299

PHILLIP ENNIS
Phillip Ennis Photography
98 Smith Street
Freeport, New York 11520
United States
Tel: (516) 379-4273

PIETER ESTERSOHN
420 East 54th Street, Room 14F
New York, New York 10022
United States
Tel: (212) 838-3170

PETER L. GLUCK
Peter L. Gluck and Partners
19 Union Square West
New York, New York 10003
United States
Tel: (212) 255-1876
Fax: (212) 633-0144

JANOS GRAPOW
Via Monti Parioli 21/A, Roma, Italy
Tel: 06/3244831

ALEC HEMER
626 East 20th Street, Apt. 6E
New York, New York 10009

United States
Tel: (212) 982-5090

LIZZIE HIMMEL
18 East 16th Street
New York, New York 10003
Tel: (212) 727-7445

EDUARD HUEBER
104 Sullivan Street
New York, New York 10021
United States
Tel: (212) 941-9294
Fax: (212) 941-9317

DAVID LIVINGSTON
1036 Erica Road
Mill Valley, California 94941
United States
Tel: (415) 383-0898

NORMAN MCGRATH
164 West 79th Street
New York, New York 10024
United States
Tel: (212) 799-6422
Fax: (212) 799-1285

KEITH SCOTT MORTON
KSM Photography, Inc.
39 West 29th Street
New York, New York 10001
United States
Tel: (212) 889-6643
Fax: (212) 684-2136

MICHAEL MUNDY
Michael Mundy Photographer, Inc.
25 Mercer Street
New York, New York 10013
Tel: (212) 226-4741
Fax: (212) 343-2936

MATTEO PIAZZA
Corso di Porta Ticinese 69
20123 Milan, Italy
Tel: 02/58106564
Fax: 02/58106926

GIOVANNA PIEMONTI
Piazza Emporio 16
Roma, Italy
Tel: 06/57300419

HUGO ROJAS
Hugo Rojas Photography
2020 North Main Street, #231
Los Angeles, California 90031
United States
Tel: (213) 222-8836

DAVID SABAL
Star Studios West
2805 Lebanon Avenue
El Paso, Texas 79930
United States
Tel: (800) 937-4368
Fax: (915) 778-1521

WALTER SMALLING
1541 8th Street, NW
Washington, DC 20001
United States
Tel: (202) 234-2438

TONY SOLURI
Soluri Photography
1147 W. Ohio Street
Chicago, Illinois 60622
United States
Tel: (312) 243-6580
Fax: (312) 243-7611

PAUL WARCHOL
Paul Warchol Photography
133 Mulberry Street
New York, New York 10013
Tel: (212) 274-1953
Fax: (212) 431-3461

ALAN WEINTRAUB
2325 Third Street, Suite 325A
San Francisco, California 94107
United States
Tel: (415) 553-8191
Fax: (415) 553-8192

INDEX

ACKNOWLEDGMENTS

The preparation of this book has been a combined effort in every respect, from concept to completion. There are many people to thank for their assistance, most of all, the designers, architects, and photographers who so graciously submitted their outstanding projects.

In very special ways, all our friends at PBC International have helped make this work a reality, especially our editor, Susan Kapsis. We are also extremely grateful to Daniela Graziose, projects coordinator, and Susan Trama in marketing.

Special thanks to Janna Kruse, whose knowledgeable assistance always sparkled with enthusiasm.